HAPPINESS IS ...
MANDALA
COLORING BOOK

ISBN-13: 978-1986181242
ISBN-10: 1986181243

Happiness
is...

Gazing into the
eyes of your
lover

Happiness
is....
the best
medicine

Happiness is...

Walking hand
in hand along
the shore.

Happiness
is...
A warm
hug on a cold
Winters day

Happiness
is ...

Being kind

Happiness
is ...

Snuggling up on
the sofa

Happiness
is ...
Needing each
other

Happiness is ...
What makes us
beautiful

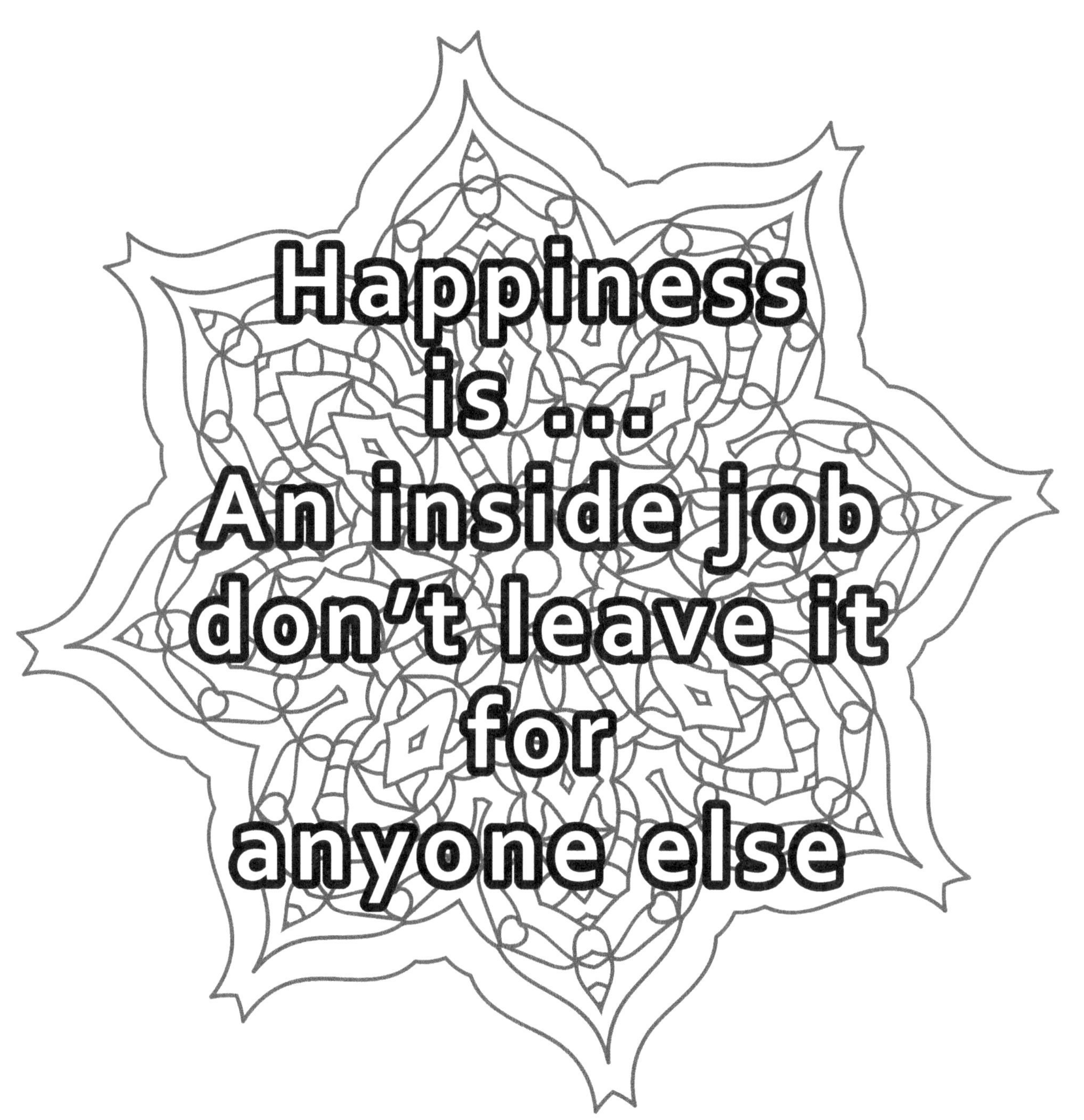

Happiness
is ...
An inside job
don't leave it
for
anyone else

Happiness
is ...

The best feeling
of all

Happiness
is ...

Seeing
the good in
everything
r

Happiness
is ...

spending your life
making each
other
smile

happiness
is ...

where
you left it

Happiness
is ...
a lovers kiss

Happiness
is ...
Making other
people happy

Happiness
is ...

Only real when
shared

Happiness
is ...

Falling in love
for the
first time

Happiness
is ...

Making
the most of
every day

Happiness
is ...

Not a goal its the
result of a well
lived life

Happiness
is ...

Finding a
rainbow in the
rain

COLOR TEST PAGE